Dr. Seuss

Agatha Christie

Ayn Rand

B Franklin

C. S. Lewis

Bertrand Russell

Booker T. Washington

Vincent

T. Carlyle

Thomas A. Edison

Rudyard Kipling

Th Jefferson

T. S. Eliot

Bacon

Mark Twain

John Wayne

Mother Teresa MC

Steven Jobs

Lincoln

Judy Garland

Anne Fran...

A. E. Hotchkiss

Albert Camus

Coco Chanel

Winston S. Churchill

W. B. Yeats

Walt Whitman

Woodrow Wilson

Theodore Roosevelt

Jonathan W...

Robert

...ther Parker

S. Hawking

Isaac

Asimov

...o Hugo

Mandela

Margaret

...jzabeth R

Martin Luther King Jr.

Inspire Me!

Mary + Patrick
Best wishes for
the holidays —
may they be
inspiring!!!
Best,
Paul James
Ginger Ayoub

Inspire Me!

A father-daughter book of quotations
to motivate, teach and inspire.

Compiled by Paul Ayoub and Lizzie Ayoub

Publisher

Michael Winston

Researcher

Meghan Kelly

Designer

Kate Terrado

Photographer

Mitch Weiss

To the two most inspiring people in my life —
my parents: Joseph Salem Ayoub and
Eleanore Maloof Ayoub.

— *Paul*

To my parents, Jane and Paul — I don't know
how I got so lucky.

— *Lizzie*

Foreword

Jane Cronin Ayoub

In the spring of 2014, Paul and I were waiting for our daughter, Lizzie, to arrive at Logan Airport in Boston. Lizzie had just completed her sophomore year at Vanderbilt University, in Nashville, Tennessee. Although we did not realize it at the time, this was to be a special homecoming.

But, first, let's rewind.

Paul was born and raised in Boston. His father, Joseph (later known to daughters-in-law, grandchildren, and friends as "Big Joe"), was the first of his family to attend college. Big Joe was an attorney. While law was the truest passion of his mind, helping others less fortunate than himself was the deepest devotion of his heart, especially in all that he did for St. Jude Children's Research Hospital. In the late 1950s, entertainer Danny Thomas reached out to Big Joe and others to help start a hospital for children suffering from catastrophic diseases. It was an easy "yes." Big Joe never forgot his roots and was inspired by the opportunity to help those who struggled in their daily lives.

Paul inherited the passion for St. Jude from both Big Joe and Paul's mother, Ellie. In the way he lives his life, it is clear that he shares their work ethic and values, never taking his blessings for granted. He followed his father's path and became a lawyer. Like his parents, Paul is deeply dedicated to St. Jude Children's Research Hospital, having served on the Board since 1992 and recently as Chairman of the Board of Governors of ALSAC, the fundraising and awareness organization for St. Jude. Paul has been inspired profoundly by his involvement with St. Jude.

This passion has now been passed on to the third generation — to Lizzie, who has been a frequent visitor to the Hospital. During one of her early visits, she met a patient, Suzanne, who touched her deeply. Soon after their meeting, Lizzie wrote a song about this extraordinary girl. She recorded the song, made and sold a CD, and donated the proceeds to St. Jude. Sadly, Suzanne did not survive, but her sweet and playful memory continues to inspire Lizzie to this day.

Now, back to that homecoming.

After the short drive home from the airport, we sat down for dinner. Lizzie asked Paul, as she so often did, what was new at St. Jude. Paul responded that his motivation to help the kids of St. Jude had only grown over the years and that he had been collecting inspirational quotes that he liked to read and reread, especially between visits to the Hospital. Lizzie, with a surprised look on her face, admitted that she also had been collecting quotes that inspired her. It didn't take long for both to decide they wanted to share these quotes that inspired, challenged, and, at times, made them laugh with others.

Inspire Me! was born.

The appearance of this symbol signifies a current or former member of the ALSAC/St. Jude Children's Research Hospital Boards of Directors and Governors or one of their national committees. In color, it denotes a member of its founding Board.

Inspire me to…

Introduction

Paul Ayoub and Lizzie Ayoub

We always have been passionate about quotations and the power they have to change attitudes, minds, and lives. Over the years, we have gathered dozens of quote books and inspirational sayings from various sources. They line our bookshelves, cover our walls, and fill our notebooks. Why are we so enamored of quotations? Perhaps, as 19th-century British Prime Minister Benjamin Disraeli once said, "The wisdom of the wise and the experience of the ages are perpetuated by quotations."

Each one of us has heard, read, or listened to words from family, friends, the famous — and the infamous — that resonate and in some way impact our lives. Words can be transformative. They can touch us in such a way as to change us and give us the ability to look at our world differently.

It is often not the words but the message behind the words that makes a quote so meaningful. Even the shortest of quotations can convey the most powerful of messages, provide meaningful perspective, and impart hard-won wisdom. In the words of 16th-century Spanish writer Miguel de Cervantes, quotations, at their core, are "short sentences drawn from long experiences."

Our family's "long experience" — in fact our family's "lifelong" experience — is rooted in our connection with St. Jude Children's Research Hospital. In 1957, our father/grandfather, Joseph Ayoub (a.k.a. "Big Joe"), met with entertainer Danny Thomas in Chicago. Danny had invited a group of first-generation Americans of Lebanese and Syrian heritage to hear about a plan he had to build a hospital in Memphis, Tennessee, for the sickest of children. From that meeting arose ALSAC, an organization formed to raise funds and awareness to support St. Jude Children's Research Hospital. Five years later, in 1962, the Hospital opened its doors with the vision of Danny Thomas that "No child should die in the dawn of life" and "No child should be denied care because of an inability to pay."

ALSAC/St. Jude Children's Research Hospital is now among the largest non-profit organizations in the United States. Today, St. Jude is leading the way the world understands, treats, and defeats childhood cancer and other life-threatening diseases. Our own passion and commitment to St. Jude motivated us to create this book and to donate all profits to the Hospital.

Danny Thomas often said, "Success has nothing to do with what you gain in life or accomplish for yourself. It's what you do for others." Much like the work that goes on at St. Jude, we hope that this collection of quotations will not only motivate and teach, but also will inspire you to inspire others. For us, that will be the measure of the success of *Inspire Me!*

Big Joe lived a life consistent with philosopher William James' saying, "The greatest use of life is to spend it for something that will outlast it." Through his service to ALSAC and St. Jude Children's Research Hospital, which began with that first meeting in 1957 and continued for the remainder of his life as a Board and Emeritus Board member, Big Joe left us with a legacy that we hope to carry on through our own continued involvement with ALSAC and St. Jude Children's Research Hospital. This book is but a small step in that journey.

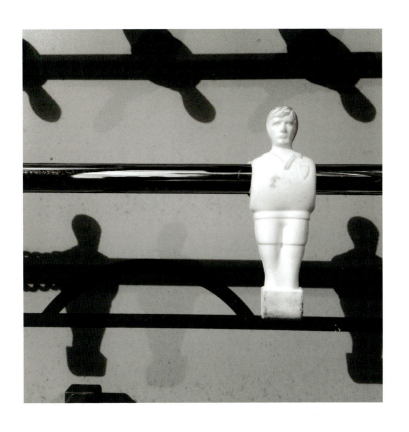

Believe in Myself

Be yourself;
everyone else is
already taken.

Oscar Wilde, *Playwright*

Everybody is a genius.
But if you judge a fish by its
ability to climb a tree,
it will live its whole life
believing that it is stupid.

Albert Einstein, *Physicist*

Where you are is a result of who you were,
but where you go depends entirely on who you
choose to be.

Hal Elrod, *Author*

Our greatest glory is not in never falling, but in
rising every time we fall.

Confucius, *Philosopher*

Believe in yourself and there will come a day when
others will have no choice but to believe with you.

Cynthia Kersey, *Author*

No one can make you feel inferior without
your consent.

Eleanor Roosevelt, *U.S. First Lady, Diplomat, and Social Activist*

The question isn't who is going to let me; it's who is
going to stop me.

Ayn Rand, *Novelist and Philosopher*

Do not let what you cannot do interfere with what you can do.

John Wooden, *College Basketball Coach*

Use what talents you possess: the woods would be very silent if no birds sang there except those that sang best.

Henry van Dyke, *Author, Educator, and Clergyman*

I think the reward for conformity is that everyone likes you except yourself.

Rita Mae Brown, *Author and Feminist Activist*

Too many people overvalue what they are not and undervalue what they are.

Malcolm Forbes, *Magazine Publisher*

The most common way people give up their power is by thinking they don't have any.

Alice Walker, *Novelist and Political Activist*

Keep your eyes on the stars, but remember to keep your feet on the ground.

Theodore Roosevelt, *U.S. President*

You have to be odd to be number one.

Dr. Seuss, *Author*

Be yourself. The world worships the original.

Ingrid Bergman, *Actress*

Never violate the sacredness of your individual self-respect.

Theodore Parker, *Unitarian Minister and Social Rights Activist*

We must not allow other people's limited perceptions to define us.

Virginia Satir, *Author and Therapist*

To be a great champion, you must believe you are the best. If you're not, pretend you are.

Muhammad Ali, *Professional Boxer*

Real difficulties can be overcome; it is the imaginary ones that are unconquerable.

Theodore Newton Vail, *Industrialist*

Aerodynamically, the bumblebee shouldn't be able to fly, but the bumblebee doesn't know it so it goes on flying anyway.

Mary Kay Ash, *Founder, Mary Kay Cosmetics*

No matter what people tell you, words and ideas can change the world.

Robin Williams, *Actor and Comedian*

Everything you need to be great is already inside you. Stop waiting for something to light your fire. You have the match.

Darren Hardy, *Motivational Speaker and Author*

Bad news is: You cannot make people like, love, understand, validate, accept, or be nice to you. You can't control them either. Good news is: It doesn't matter.

Unknown

Life isn't about finding yourself. Life is about creating yourself.

George Bernard Shaw, *Playwright*

Consult not your fears, but your hopes and your dreams.

Pope John XXIII

No price is too high to pay for the privilege of owning yourself.

Friedrich Nietzsche, *Philosopher*

Accept responsibility for your life. Know that it is you who will get you where you want to go, no one else.

Les Brown, *Motivational Speaker*

Do not fear to be eccentric in opinion, for every opinion now accepted was once eccentric.

Bertrand Russell, *Philosopher and Mathematician*

Never face the facts or you won't even get out of bed in the morning. The facts – polls, statistics, conventional wisdom – *can keep anyone from starting anything.* Better to **create your own** facts.

Marlo Thomas, *National Outreach Director, St. Jude Children's Research Hospital, Actress, Author, and Humanitarian*

I ask not for a *lighter burden*, but for *broader shoulders*.

Jewish Proverb

Confidence sells — people believe in those who believe in themselves.

Simon Black, *Investor and Entrepreneur*

Do what you feel in your heart to be right — for you will be criticized anyway.

Eleanor Roosevelt, *U.S. First Lady, Diplomat, and Social Activist*

Never give up on what you really want to do. The person with big dreams is more powerful than one with all the facts.

Albert Einstein, *Physicist*

If my mind can conceive it and my heart can believe it — then I can achieve it.

Muhammad Ali, *Professional Boxer*

One has to understand that braveness is not the absence of fear, but rather the strength to keep on going forward despite the fear.

Paulo Coelho, *Novelist*

Courage is the resistance of fear, mastery of fear —
not absence of fear.

Mark Twain, *Novelist*

Laugh at yourself first before anyone else can.

Elsa Maxwell, *Gossip Columnist*

Don't ask yourself what the world needs. Ask
yourself what makes you come alive and then go do
that. Because what the world needs is people who
have come alive.

Howard Thurman, *Minister and Civil Rights Activist*

Most people are mirror people. They only reflect
how others treat them. Be a flashlight person and
always shine no matter what.

Salem Abraham, *Investment Manager*

A great pleasure in life is doing what people say you
cannot do.

Walter Bagehot, *Journalist*

Courage is being scared to death but saddling
up anyway.

John Wayne, *Actor*

When I entered the upper school I felt lonely — at
the bottom of the heap. There was one girl who
made me feel miserable. She was mean and critical
of everything I said or did. She was in all my
classes and seemed to lurk in every corner of the
school. Eventually I mustered up the courage to tell
her to stop. And she did stop. And you know who
that girl was? I was that girl. I had been hard on
myself and unforgiving, so I decided to just be me
with a heart for any fate!

Katherine Kirk, *High School Student President*

Depend not on another, but lean instead on thyself.
True happiness is born of self-reliance.

The Laws of Manu, *Ancient Hindu Text*

If you don't have confidence, you'll always find a
way not to win.

Carl Lewis, *Olympic Track and Field Athlete*

Never apologize for having high standards. People who really want to be in your life will rise up to meet them.

Ziad K. Abdelnour, *Financier*

It always seems impossible until it's done.

Nelson Mandela, *President of South Africa*

Beauty begins the moment you decide to be yourself.

Coco Chanel, *Fashion Designer*

You cannot be lonely if you like the person you are alone with.

Wayne Dyer, *Motivational Speaker and Author*

The beautiful thing about fear is, when you run to it, it runs away.

Robin S. Sharma, *Writer*

The only thing that stands between you and your dream is the will to try and the belief that it is actually possible.

Joel Brown, *Writer*

Always be a first-rate version of yourself and not a second-rate version of someone else.

Judy Garland, *Singer and Actress*

Ever tried. Ever failed. No Matter. Try again. Fail Again. Fail better.

Samuel Beckett, *Playwright*

It is hard to beat a person who never gives up.

Babe Ruth, *Professional Baseball Player*

What we first find impossible, we later deem unlikely, and eventually accept as inevitable.

William Bennett, *U.S. Secretary of Education*

Seize the Moment

The reason so many people *never get anywhere in life* is because when opportunity knocks, they are out in the backyard *looking for four-leaf clovers.*

Walter Chrysler, *Founder, Chrysler Corporation*

You can destroy your **now** worrying about **tomorrow.**

Janis Joplin, *Singer and Songwriter*

A journey of a thousand miles begins with a single step.

Lao Tzu, *Philosopher*

Live as if you were to die tomorrow. Learn as if you were to live forever.

Mahatma Gandhi, *Indian Political and Spiritual Leader*

Don't let yesterday use up too much of today.

Cherokee Proverb

Why be a dreamer when you can wake up and make it reality?

Larissa May, *Blogger and Founder of @halfthestory*

Age wrinkles the body. Quitting wrinkles the soul.

Douglas MacArthur, *U.S. Army General*

You'll never plough a field by turning it over in your mind.

Irish Proverb

Somewhere, something incredible is waiting to be known.

Carl Sagan, *Astronomer*

Either define the moment or the moment will define you.

Walt Whitman, *Poet*

Most look up and admire the stars. A champion climbs a mountain and grabs one.

Unknown

Doing the best at this moment puts you in the best place for the next moment.

Oprah Winfrey, *Talk Show Host, Philanthropist, and Actress*

You can't build a reputation on what you're going to do.

Henry Ford, *Founder, Ford Motor Company*

Do not wait to strike 'till the iron is hot; but make it hot by striking.

W.B. Yeats, *Poet*

The fox fears not the man who boasts by night but the man who rises early in the morning.

Gary Player, *Professional Golfer*

You don't have to be great to start, but you have to start to be great.

Zig Ziglar, *Motivational Speaker and Author*

You may delay, but time will not.

Benjamin Franklin, *Statesman and Inventor*

Life is short, break the rules. Forgive quickly, kiss slowly. Love truly. Laugh uncontrollably and never regret anything that makes you smile.

Mark Twain, *Novelist*

Let us not look back in anger, nor forward in fear, but around us in awareness.

James Thurber, *Cartoonist and Journalist*

You've gotta dance like there's nobody watching, love like you'll never be hurt, sing like there's nobody listening, and live like it's heaven on earth.

William W. Purkey, *Writer and Educator*

Opportunities will come and go, but if you do nothing about them, so will you.

Richie Norton, *Author*

Create moments and not memories.

Nicole E. Hajjar, *Music Publicist*

It is never too late to start living the life you wish you had.

Lailah Gifty Akita, *Author and Social Activist*

Whether you think you can or think you can't, you are right.

Henry Ford, *Founder, Ford Motor Company*

A lot of what we ascribe to luck is not luck at all. It's seizing the day and accepting responsibility for your future.

Howard Schultz, *Founder and CEO, Starbucks*

Yesterday is history. Tomorrow is a mystery. Today is a gift.

Eleanor Roosevelt, *U.S. First Lady, Diplomat, and Social Activist*

Today I will do what others won't, so tomorrow I can accomplish what others can't.

Jerry Rice, *Professional Football Player*

I hear people talk a lot about what they are going to do and rarely see them actually do it. When in doubt, DO something.

Mark Crandall, *Banker*

The secret of **getting ahead**
is *getting started*.

Mark Twain, *Novelist*

Whenever you are asked if
you can do a job, tell 'em,
"Certainly I can!"
Then get busy and find
out how to do it.

Theodore Roosevelt, *U.S. President*

The saddest summary of a life contains three descriptions: could have, might have, and should have.

Louis E. Boone, *Author*

You can't change the past, but you can ruin the present by worrying about the future.

Unknown

Tomorrow is often the busiest day of the year.

Spanish Proverb

Go for it now. The future is promised to no one.

Wayne Dyer, *Motivational Speaker and Author*

If opportunity doesn't knock, build a door.

Milton Berle, *Comedian*

Keep your fears to yourself, but share your courage with others.

Robert Louis Stevenson, *Novelist*

The way to get started is to quit talking and begin doing.

Walt Disney, *Co-Founder, The Walt Disney Company*

Show me a person who never made a mistake, and I will show you a person who never did anything.

William Rosenberg, *Entrepreneur*

It had long since come to my attention that people of accomplishment rarely sat back and let things happen to them. They went out and happened to things.

Leonardo da Vinci, *Artist and Inventor*

A wise man will make more opportunities than he finds.

Francis Bacon, *Philosopher and Essayist*

The only disability in life is a bad attitude.

Scott Hamilton, *Professional Figure Skater*

You'll never find a rainbow if you're looking down.

Charlie Chaplin, *Actor and Filmmaker*

It is never too late to be what you might have been.

George Eliot, *Novelist*

Life is a great big canvas, and you should throw all the paint you can on it.

Danny Kaye, *Entertainer*

Take Risks

If no one ever took *risks*, Michelangelo would have painted the Sistine floor.

Neil Simon, *Playwright*

Behold the turtle. He only makes progress when he sticks his neck out.

James Bryant Conant, *Harvard University President and U.S. Ambassador*

Faith is taking the first step even when you don't see the whole staircase.

Martin Luther King, Jr., *Civil Rights Leader*

If you aren't in over your head, how do you know how tall you are?

T.S. Eliot, *Poet*

If I had my life to live again, I'd make the same mistakes, only sooner.

Tallulah Bankhead, *Actress*

To escape criticism — do nothing, say nothing, and be nothing.

Elbert G. Hubbard, *Writer and Artist*

Twenty years from now you will be more disappointed by the things you didn't do than by the ones you did.

Mark Twain, *Novelist*

Don't be afraid to go out on a limb. That's where the fruit is.

H. Jackson Brown, Jr., *Author*

Only those who dare to fail greatly can ever achieve greatly.

Robert F. Kennedy, *U.S. Attorney General and Senator*

If you have the freedom to fly, don't be afraid to fall.

Larissa May, *Blogger and Founder of @halfthestory*

Life is inherently risky. There is only one big risk you should avoid at all costs, and that is the risk of doing nothing.

Denis Waitley, *Motivational Speaker and Author*

Of all the liars in the world, sometimes the worst are your own fears.

Rudyard Kipling, *Novelist and Poet*

Failure means nothing unless you let it.

Tom Penn, *Sports Executive*

The greatest mistake you can make in life is to be continually fearing you will make one.

Elbert G. Hubbard, *Writer and Artist*

To avoid situations in which you might make mistakes may be the greatest mistake of all.

Peter McWilliams, *Author*

When you take risks you learn that there will be times when you succeed and there will be times when you fail, and both are equally important.

Ellen DeGeneres, *Comedian and Television Host*

Only those who will risk going too far can possibly find out how far one can go.

T.S. Eliot, *Poet*

There are risks and costs to a program of action.
But they are far less than the long-range risks and
costs of comfortable inaction.

John F. Kennedy, *U.S. President*

We must all suffer one of two things: the pain of
discipline or the pain of regret or disappointment.

Jim Rohn, *Motivational Author and Speaker*

You miss 100% of the shots you don't take.

Wayne Gretsky, *Professional Hockey Player*

The bitterest tears shed over graves are for words
unsaid and deeds left undone.

Harriet Beecher Stowe, *Novelist and Abolitionist*

Anything I've ever done that ultimately was
worthwhile initially scared me to death.

Betty Bender, *Business Consultant*

What haunts me far more than anything I've ever done are the things I haven't done.

Dan Pearce, *Author and Artist*

The man who is afraid to risk failure seldom has to face success.

John Wooden, *College Basketball Coach*

Don't be too timid and squeamish about your actions. All life is an experiment. The more experiments you make the better.

Ralph Waldo Emerson, *Essayist and Poet*

It's fine to celebrate success, but it is more important to heed the lessons of failure.

Bill Gates, *Co-Founder, Microsoft and Philanthropist*

Failure is unimportant. It takes courage to make a fool of yourself.

Charlie Chaplin, *Actor and Filmmaker*

Life is about *failing* and **success** is the *rebound*.

Larissa May, *Blogger and Founder of @halfthestory*

Risk more than others think is safe. **Care more** than others think is wise. **Dream more** than others think is practical. **Expect more** than others think is possible.

Claude Bissell, *Educator and Author*

Never regret. If it's good, it's wonderful. If it's bad, it's experience.

Victoria Holt, *Author*

What would you attempt to do if you knew you could not fail?

Robert H. Schuller, *Christian Televangelist and Author*

Sometimes your only available transportation is a leap of faith.

Margaret Shepherd, *Calligrapher and Author*

Adapt and Change

The real voyage of
discovery consists not in
seeking new landscapes but
in *having new eyes.*

Marcel Proust, *Novelist*

If the only tool you have is
a **hammer**, you tend to see
every problem as a **nail**.

Abraham Maslow, *Psychologist*

No man ever steps in the same river twice, for it's not the same river, and he's not the same man.

Heraclitus, *Philosopher*

Life isn't about waiting for the storm to pass. It's about learning to dance in the rain.

Vivian Greene, *Author and Artist*

In times of rapid change, experience could be your worst enemy.

J. Paul Getty, *Industrialist*

We know what happens to people who stay in the middle of the road. They get run over.

Aneurin Bevan, *Member of British Parliament*

When the winds of change blow, some people build walls and others build windmills.

Chinese Proverb

When one door closes another door opens; but we so often look so long and so regretfully upon the closed door that we do not see the ones which open for us.

Alexander Graham Bell, *Inventor*

The most dangerous phrase in the language is, "We've always done it this way."

Grace Hopper, *U.S. Navy Rear Admiral*

Progress lies not in enhancing what is, but in advancing toward what will be.

Khalil Gibran, *Poet and Philosopher*

When you are finished changing, you're finished.

Benjamin Franklin, *Statesman and Inventor*

Your assumptions are your windows on the world. Scrub them off every once in a while or the light won't come in.

Alan Alda, *Actor*

Things turn out best for the people who make the best of the way things turn out.

John Wooden, *College Basketball Coach*

To improve is to change; to be perfect is to change often.

Winston Churchill, *U.K. Prime Minister*

It is not the strongest or the most intelligent who will survive but those who can best manage change.

Attributed to Charles Darwin, *Scientist*

God changes not what is in a people, until they change what is in themselves.

Quran (13:11)

Failure is not fatal, but failure to change might be.

John Wooden, *College Basketball Coach*

Progress is impossible without change, and those who cannot change their minds cannot change anything.

George Bernard Shaw, *Playwright*

No sensible decision can be made any longer without taking into account not only the world as it is, but the world as it will be.

Isaac Asimov, *Science Fiction Writer*

Intelligence is the ability to adapt to change.

Stephen Hawking, *Scientist*

Change is the law of life. And those who look only to the past or present are certain to miss the future.

John F. Kennedy, *U.S. President*

There is nothing permanent except change.

Heraclitus, *Philosopher*

The world hates change, yet it is the only thing that has brought progress.

Charles F. Kettering, *Businessman and Inventor*

May your choices reflect your hopes, not your fears.

Nelson Mandela, *President of South Africa*

Change is the price of survival.

Winston Churchill, *U.K. Prime Minister*

Progress is a nice word. But change is its motivator. And change has its enemies.

Robert F. Kennedy, *U.S. Senator and Attorney General*

Where there is no vision, the people perish.

Proverbs 29:18

If you do what you've always done, you'll get what you've always gotten.

Tony Robbins, *Motivational Speaker and Author*

Even the most powerful person on earth **can't change yesterday.** But all of us can *change what we do today.* And that's how we ***change all of our tomorrows.***

Robert Reynolds, *Business Executive*

We cannot direct the *wind*, but we can adjust the *sails*.

Dolly Parton, *Singer and Songwriter*

If you feel like it's difficult to change, you will probably have a harder time succeeding.

Andrea Jung, *Business Executive*

If we don't change, we don't grow. If we don't grow, we aren't really living.

Gail Sheehy, *Author*

A good hockey player plays where the puck is. A great hockey player plays where the puck is going to be.

Wayne Gretzky, *Professional Hockey Player*

Conformity is that jailer of freedom and the enemy of growth.

John F. Kennedy, *U.S. President*

Your life does not get better by chance. It gets better by change.

Jim Rohm, *Motivational Author and Speaker*

I would rather learn to dance in the rain, than worry if I have an umbrella for the rest of my life.

James N. Rowe, *U.S. Army Officer and Author*

The fastest way to change yourself is to hang out with people who are already the way you want to be.

Reid Hoffman, *Co-Founder, LinkedIn*

Yesterday I was clever, so I wanted to change the world. Today I am wise, so I am changing myself.

Jalal ad-Din Rumi, *Poet*

Everybody has a plan, until they get punched in the face.

Mike Tyson, *Professional Boxer*

Don't spend time beating on a wall hoping to transform it into a door.

Coco Chanel, *Fashion Designer*

The first step towards getting somewhere is to decide that you are not going to stay where you are.

J.P. Morgan, *Financier*

Be most interested in finding the best way, not having your own way.

John Wooden, *College Basketball Coach*

Teach thy tongue to say "I do not know," and thou shalt progress.

Maimonides, *Philosopher and Scholar*

If you hit a wrong note, then make it right by what you play afterwards.

Joe Pass, *Musician*

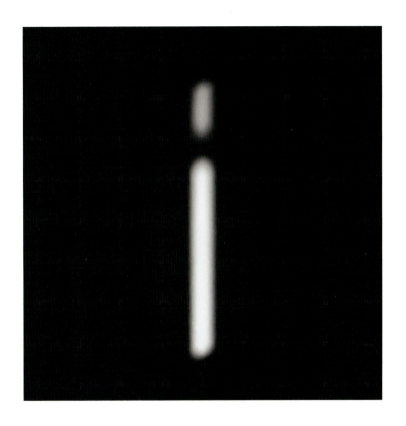

Have Wisdom

The *butterfly* often forgets it
once *was a caterpillar*.

Swedish Proverb

Never allow a person
to tell you no who doesn't
have the *power to say yes*.

Eleanor Roosevelt, *U.S. First Lady, Diplomat, and Social Activist*

Courage is what it takes to stand up and speak;
courage is also what it takes to sit down and listen.

Winston Churchill, *U.K. Prime Minister*

I am not young enough to know everything.

Oscar Wilde, *Playwright*

It is easy to walk through the forest once someone
has cut down the trees.

Joseph R. Shaker, *Advertising Agency Owner*

Experience is a hard teacher because she gives the
test first, the lesson afterwards.

Vern Law, *Professional Baseball Player*

There is nothing wrong with having nothing to
say — unless you insist on saying it.

Ralph Waldo Emerson, *Essayist and Poet*

Common sense is the least common of all the senses.

Mark Twain, *Novelist*

If you and I agreed on everything, they'd only need one of us.

Joseph R. Shaker, *Advertising Agency Owner*

I not only use all the brains I have, but all I can borrow.

Woodrow Wilson, *U.S. President*

No man ever listened himself out of a job.

Calvin Coolidge, *U.S. President*

God gives us nuts, but he does not crack them for us.

German Proverb

Life… is a process of living.

Louis Chow, *Physician and Cancer Survivor*

The most important thing in communication is to hear what isn't being said.

Peter Drucker, *Management Consultant and Author*

The true test of a person's character is how they treat the people in life that they don't need.

Lee Corso, *College Football Coach*

Among my most prized possessions are the words that I have never spoken.

Orson Scott Card, *Author*

The larger the island of knowledge, the longer the shoreline of wonder.

Ralph W. Sockman, *Protestant Clergyman*

The truth is like the sun, hard to look at, but you cannot live without it.

Fred P. Gattas, Jr., *Business Executive*

Wisdom is the reward you get for a lifetime of listening when you'd have preferred to talk.

Doug Larson, *Journalist*

When love and skill work together, expect
a masterpiece.

John Ruskin, *Art Critic*

He who knows others is learned. He who knows
himself is wise.

Lao Tzu, *Philosopher*

Human progress never rolls in on the wheels
of inevitability.

Martin Luther King, Jr., *Civil Rights Leader*

Be more concerned with your character than your
reputation, because your character is what you
really are, while your reputation is merely what
others think you are.

John Wooden, *College Basketball Coach*

In any situation, the best thing you can do is the
right thing; the next best thing you can do is the
wrong thing; the worst thing you can do is nothing.

Theodore Roosevelt, *U.S. President*

Character is much easier kept than recovered.

Thomas Paine, *Political Activist and Theorist*

Be a good listener. Your ears will never get you in trouble.

Frank Tyger, *Cartoonist*

Don't let your failures define you — let them teach you.

Barack Obama, *U.S. President*

We do not see things as they are. We see them as we are.

Unknown

Well done is better than well said.

Benjamin Franklin, *Statesman and Inventor*

When you listen, it's amazing what you can learn. When you act on what you've learned, it's amazing what you can change.

Audrey McLaughlin, *Member of Canadian Parliament*

Knowledge *speaks,*
but **wisdom** *listens.*

Jimi Hendrix, *Singer and Songwriter*

Wise men talk because they
have *something to say;*
fools, because they have to
say something.

Plato, *Philosopher*

Never say you're sorry unless you really mean it.

Cosmo Macero, Jr., *Public Relations and Communications Consultant*

Before you speak, listen. Before you spend, earn. Before you criticize, wait. Before leaving, try.

William Arthur Ward, *Author*

Real knowledge is to know the extent of one's ignorance.

Confucius, *Philosopher*

All men make mistakes, but only wise men learn from their mistakes.

Winston Churchill, *U.K. Prime Minister*

There will come a time when you believe everything is finished. That will be the beginning.

Louis L'Amour, *Author*

I've never learned anything while I was talking.

Larry King, *Television Host*

Whatever is begun in anger ends in shame.

Benjamin Franklin, *Statesman and Inventor*

It takes a great man to be a good listener.

Calvin Coolidge, *U.S. President*

Seek first to understand, then to be understood.

Stephen Covey, *Management Consultant and Author*

**Forgive your enemies, but never forget
their names.**

John F. Kennedy, *U.S. President*

**Speak when you are angry and you will make the
best speech you will ever regret.**

Ambrose Bierce, *Satirist*

**All of us invent ourselves. Some of us just have
more imagination than others.**

Cher, *Singer and Actress*

The best way to destroy an enemy is to make him
a friend.

Abraham Lincoln, *U.S. President*

The secret of a man who is universally interesting is
that he is universally interested.

William Dean Howells, *Novelist*

There is no evil like hatred. And no fortitude
like patience.

Shantideva, *Buddhist Monk*

In the frank expression of conflicting opinions lies the
greatest promise of wisdom in government action.

Louis Brandeis, *U.S. Supreme Court Justice*

There's a time to spend and a time to save.

Eleanore Ayoub, *Mother and Grandmother*

There is only one pretty child in the world and every mother has it.

Chinese Proverb

Rock bottom became the solid foundation on which I rebuilt my life.

J.K. Rowling, *Novelist*

Listening, not imitation, may be the sincerest form of flattery.

Joyce Brothers, *Psychologist*

The most important ability is accountability.

Shawn Sullivan, *Sports Executive*

Character, like a photograph, develops in darkness.

Yousuf Karsh, *Photographer*

It is the province of knowledge to speak and it is the privilege of wisdom to listen.

Oliver Wendell Holmes, Sr., *Physician and Author*

There is nothing so annoying as to have two people go right on talking when you're interrupting.

Mark Twain, *Novelist*

The graveyards are full with indispensible men.

Charles de Gaulle, *President of France*

Succeed

Not knowing when the
dawn will come
I open every door.

Emily Dickinson, *Poet*

It is important
to **think big,**
but you've got
to ***work small.***

Marlo Thomas, *National Outreach Director, St. Jude Children's Research Hospital, Actress, Author, and Humanitarian*

Opportunity is missed by most people because it is dressed in overalls and looks like work.

Thomas Edison, *Inventor*

I am a slow walker, but I never walk back.

Abraham Lincoln, *U.S. President*

The temptation to quit will be greatest just before you are about to succeed.

Bob Parsons, *Businessman*

Ambition beats genius ninety-nine percent of the time.

Jay Leno, *Comedian*

If you really want to do something, you'll find a way. If you don't, you'll find an excuse.

Jim Rohn, *Motivational Author and Speaker*

If you fail to prepare you are preparing to fail.

Benjamin Franklin, *Statesman and Inventor*

Luck is what happens when preparation meets opportunity.

Attributed to Seneca, *Philosopher*

I attribute my success to this — I never gave or took any excuse.

Florence Nightingale, *Founder of Modern Nursing*

The best preparation for tomorrow is to do today's work superbly well.

William Osler, *Physician and Educator*

Chance favors the prepared mind. The more you practice, the luckier you become.

Richard Branson, *Businessman*

The only place success comes before work is in the dictionary.

Vince Lombardi, *College Football Coach*

What we hope ever to do with ease, we must learn to first do with diligence.

Samuel Johnson, *Essayist and Poet*

I have never known a really successful man who deep in his heart did not understand the grind, the discipline it takes to win.

Vince Lombardi, *College Football Coach*

Keep your head down, work hard, and good things will come your way.

Paul Nasser, *Real Estate Executive*

We all have ability. The difference is how we use it.

Stevie Wonder, *Musician*

Keep on going and the chances are you will stumble on something, perhaps when you are least expecting it. I have never heard of anyone stumbling on something sitting down.

Charles F. Kettering, *Businessman and Inventor*

Excellence is the gradual result of always striving to do better.

Pat Riley, *Professional Basketball Player and Coach*

Nothing will work unless you do.

Maya Angelou, *Poet*

Success is the sum of small efforts, repeated day-in and day-out.

Robert Collier, *Author*

It does not matter how slowly you go as long as you do not stop.

Confucius, *Philosopher*

Never confuse a single defeat with a final defeat.

F. Scott Fitzgerald, *Novelist*

Never interrupt someone doing what you said couldn't be done.

Amelia Earhart, *Aviation Pioneer and Author*

There may be people that have more talent than you, but there's no excuse for anyone to work harder than you do.

Derek Jeter, *Professional Baseball Player*

Genius is one percent inspiration and ninety-nine percent perspiration.

Thomas Edison, *Inventor*

Results, not process! Never let the journey of process be an excuse for lack of results.

Paul Ayoub, *Attorney*

It is better to be prepared for an opportunity and not have one, than to have an opportunity and not be prepared.

Whitney Young, *Civil Rights Activist*

It is not enough to stay busy. So, too, are the ants. The question is what you are busy about.

Henry David Thoreau, *Author and Philosopher*

If I had **eight** hours to chop down a tree, I would spend **six** hours sharpening my axe.

Abraham Lincoln, *U.S. President*

The block of granite which was an **obstacle** in the pathway of the *weak*, became a **stepping-stone** in the pathway of the *strong*.

Thomas Carlyle, *Philosopher and Historian*

Once you learn to quit, it becomes a habit.

Vince Lombardi, *College Football Coach*

Don't be mislead by the waves on top of the water; focus on the direction of the current underneath.

Tom Penn, *Sports Executive*

There are no secrets to success. It is the result of preparation, hard work, and learning from failure.

Colin Powell, *U.S. Army General and Secretary of State*

Be so good they can't ignore you.

Steve Martin, *Comedian and Actor*

Discipline is the bridge between goals and accomplishment.

Jim Rohn, *Motivational Author and Speaker*

Be like a duck, my mother used to tell me. Remain calm on the surface and paddle like hell underneath.

Michael Caine, *Actor*

Defeat is simply a signal to press onward.

Helen Keller, *Author and Activist*

The difference in winning and losing is most often not quitting.

Walt Disney, *Co-Founder, The Walt Disney Company*

Great things are not done by impulse, but by a series of small things brought together.

Vincent van Gogh, *Artist*

Ninety-nine percent of all failures come from people who have a habit of making excuses.

George Washington Carver, *Scientist*

Success in life comes not from holding a good hand, but in playing a poor hand well.

Denis Waitley, *Businessman*

Ambition is the path to success. Persistence is the vehicle you arrive in.

Bill Bradley, *Professional Basketball Player and U.S. Senator*

Never look back unless you are planning to go
that way.

Henry David Thoreau, *Author and Philosopher*

The harder you work, the harder it is to surrender.

Vince Lombardi, *College Football Coach*

Victory has a hundred fathers and defeat is
an orphan.

Count Galeazzo Ciano, *Italian Diplomat*

It is more difficult to stay on top than to get there.

Mia Hamm, *Professional Soccer Player*

You may have to fight a battle more than once
to win it.

Margaret Thatcher, *U.K. Prime Minister*

You must have long-term goals to keep you from
being frustrated by short-term failures.

Charles C. Noble, *U.S. Army Major General*

In business, success means hearing "no," and converting it to "yes."

Paul Ayoub, *Attorney*

The perils of overwork are slight compared with the dangers of inactivity.

Thomas Edison, *Inventor*

Strength does not come from physical capacity. It comes from an indomitable will.

Mahatma Gandhi, *Indian Political and Spiritual Leader*

Accomplishments will prove to be a journey, not a destination.

Dwight D. Eisenhower, *U.S. President*

I know the price of success: dedication, hard work, and an unremitting devotion to the things you want to see happen.

Frank Lloyd Wright, *Architect*

Hard work spotlights the character of people: some turn up their sleeves, some turn up their noses, and some don't turn up at all.

Sam Ewing, *Professional Baseball Player*

We are what we repeatedly do. Excellence, then, is not an act but a habit.

Aristotle, *Philosopher*

A successful man is one who can lay a firm foundation with the bricks others have thrown at him.

David Brinkley, *Journalist and Newscaster*

The person who sends out positive thoughts activates the world around him positively and draws back to himself positive results.

Norman Vincent Peale, *Author*

There are no traffic jams along the extra mile.

Roger Staubach, *Professional Football Player and Businessman*

Successful people are always looking for opportunities to help others. Unsuccessful people are always asking, "What's in it for me?"

Dwight D. Eisenhower, *U.S. President*

Tact is the knack of making a point without making an enemy.

Isaac Newton, *Physicist and Mathematician*

Who are you going to be in the world ... and how great are you willing to have it?

Judy Habib, *Brand Strategist*

Many of life's failures are people who did not realize how close they were to success when they gave up.

Thomas Edison, *Inventor*

People forget how fast you did a job, but they remember how well you did it.

Howard Newton, *Musician*

All things are difficult before they are easy.

Thomas Fuller, *Writer*

You never know what's around the corner. It could be everything. Or it could be nothing. You keep putting one foot in front of the other and then one day you look back and you've climbed a mountain.

Tom Hiddleston, *Actor*

If you're going through hell, keep going.

Winston Churchill, *U.K. Prime Minister*

If you don't have critics, you probably don't have success either.

Nicki Minaj, *Singer and Songwriter*

If you ever see a turtle on a fence post, you know it didn't get there by itself.

Unknown

Live with Purpose

Success has *nothing* to do with *what you gain* in life *or accomplish* for yourself. **It's what you do for others.**

Danny Thomas, *Founder, St. Jude Children's Research Hospital, Entertainer, and Humanitarian*

The biggest human temptation is to *settle for too little.*

Thomas Merton, *Trappist Monk*

The two most important days of your life are the day you were born, and the day you find out why.

Mark Twain, *Novelist*

He who walks in another's tracks leaves no footprints.

Joan Brannon, *Writer*

It seems the harder I work, the more luck I have.

Thomas Jefferson, *U.S. President*

We all live with the objective of being happy; our lives are all different and yet the same.

Anne Frank, *Diarist*

Obstacles are those frightful things you see when you take your eyes off the goal.

Henry Ford, *Founder, Ford Motor Company*

Don't judge each day by the harvest you reap but by the seeds you plant.

Robert Louis Stevenson, *Novelist*

When you were born, you cried and the world rejoiced. Live your life so that when you die, the world cries and you rejoice.

Native American Proverb

It is not only for what we do that we are held responsible, but also for what we do not do.

Molière, *Playwright*

Your time is limited, don't waste it living someone else's life.

Steve Jobs, *Co-Founder and CEO, Apple Inc.*

It's not the years in your life but the life in your years that counts.

Adlai Stevenson II, *Illinois Governor and U.S. Ambassador*

Measure your life through love, not likes.

Larissa May, *Blogger and Founder of @halfthestory*

He who denies his heritage has no heritage.

Khalil Gibran, *Poet and Philosopher*

Enjoy all that you have while pursuing all
you want.

Jim Rohn, *Motivational Author and Speaker*

What you are is God's gift to you, what you become
is your gift to God.

Han Urs von Balthasar, *Theologian and Priest*

Don't let good luck become your adopted policy.

Tom Penn, *Sports Executive*

Far and away the best prize that life offers is the
chance to work hard at work worth doing.

Thomas Jefferson, *U.S. President*

Never accept the unacceptable, never tolerate the
intolerable, and when you see injustice, speak up
regardless of what personal price you might pay.

Mark Wein, *Holocaust Survivor*

In my experience, humility and gratitude are the only paths to grace. And grace is a pretty good destination to have.

Ruth Gaviria, *Marketing Executive*

Experience is what you get when you don't get what you want.

Randy Pausch, *Professor*

Efforts and courage are not enough without purpose and direction.

John F. Kennedy, *U.S. President*

Here is a test to find out whether your mission in life is complete. If you are alive, it isn't.

Lauren Bacall, *Actress*

An old man was relating his story to his children and said, "There have always been three elements to life: space, money, and time. Unlike space and money, time is unidirectional: it gets spent, it never comes back."

Gabriel Haddad, *Physician and Professor*

To forget one's purpose is the commonest form of stupidity.

Friedrich Nietzsche, *Philosopher*

May you live all the days of your life.

Jonathan Swift, *Satirist and Poet*

The goal of every human life lies in being more, not simply having more.

Pope John Paul II, *Roman Catholic Saint*

Luck is the residue of design.

Branch Rickey, *Baseball Executive*

He who has a why to live for can bear almost any how.

Friedrich Nietzsche, *Philosopher*

It's nice to be important, but it's more important to be nice.

Attributed to Thomas P. O'Neill, Sr., *Co-Founder, the Bricklayers Union of America and father of House Speaker Thomas P. O'Neill, Jr.*

You only live once,

but if you **do it right**,

once is enough.

Mae West, *Actress*

Always stand on **principle**…

even if you stand alone.

John Adams, *U.S. President*

And though I have the gift of prophecy, and understand all mysteries, and all knowledge; and though I have all faith, so that I could remove mountains, and have not charity, I am nothing.

1 Corinthians 13:2

It is so much easier sometimes to sit down and be resigned than to rise up and be indignant.

Nellie Letitia McClung, *Author and Social Activist*

Do not go where the path may lead, go instead where there is no path and leave a trail.

Ralph Waldo Emerson, *Essayist and Poet*

It is better to be a failure at something you love than to be a success at something you hate.

George Burns, *Comedian and Actor*

You are never too old to set another goal or to dream a new dream.

C.S. Lewis, *Novelist and Literary Critic*

We can't do much about the length of our lives, but we can do plenty about its width and depth.

Evan Escar, *Humorist*

Every day do something that will inch you closer to a better tomorrow.

Doug Firebaugh, *Author and Radio Personality*

Hit the ball over the fence and you can take your time going around the bases.

John W. Raper, *Columnist*

Motivation is a fire from within. If someone else tries to light that fire under you, chances are it will burn very briefly.

Stephen Covey, *Management Consultant and Author*

It is good to have an end to journey toward, but it is the journey that matters in the end.

Ernest Hemingway, *Novelist*

The great thing in this world is not so much where we are but in what direction we are moving.

Oliver Wendell Holmes, Sr., *Physician and Author*

You've got to get up every morning with determination if you're going to go to bed with satisfaction.

George Horace Lorimer, *Editor and Author*

The grand essentials to happiness in this life are something to do, something to love, and something to hope for.

George Washington Burnap, *Clergyman*

It's the possibility of having a dream come true that makes life interesting.

Paulo Coelho, *Novelist*

I have a job, but I don't work.

Kevin Phelan, *Real Estate Executive*

Look to the future, because that is where you'll spend the rest of your life.

George Burns, *Comedian and Actor*

Make the most of yourself by fanning the tiny, inner sparks of possibility into flames of achievement.

Golda Meir, *Prime Minister of Israel*

Enjoy the little things in life, for one day you may look back and realize they were the big things.

Robert Brault, *Writer*

As human beings, our greatness lies not so much in being able to remake the world… as in being able to remake ourselves.

Mahatma Gandhi, *Indian Political and Spiritual Leader*

If you cannot do great things, do small things in a great way.

Napoleon Hill, *Author*

Time seems short when one tries to achieve a goal, but every minute feels like a day when you are enjoying your achievements.

Mahir Awdeh, *Physician*

Stones in the road? I save every single one and one day I'll build a castle.

Fernando Pessoa, *Poet*

Inspire Others

In the end, we will remember not the words of our enemies, but the *silence of our friends*.

Martin Luther King, Jr., *Civil Rights Leader*

Being **powerful** is like being a lady. If you have to tell people you are, you *aren't*.

Margaret Thatcher, *U.K. Prime Minister*

When spider webs unite, they can tie up a lion.

Ethiopian Proverb

When you do the common things in life in an uncommon way, you will command the attention of the world.

George Washington Carver, *Scientist*

He didn't tell me how to live; he lived, and let me watch him do it.

Clarence Budington Kelland, *Author*

Never, never, never — in nothing great or small, large or petty — never give in except to convictions of honor and good sense.

Winston Churchill, *U.K. Prime Minister*

To lead people, walk behind them.

Lao Tzu, *Philosopher*

Feed the winners, fix the losers, and leave the broad middle alone.

David Karam, *Business Executive*

A goal without a plan is just a wish.

Antoine de Saint-Exupéry, *Author and Aviator*

A single leaf working alone provides no shade.

Chuck Page, *California Public Official*

Try to become not a man of success, but try rather to become a man of value.

Albert Einstein, *Physicist*

Never confuse motion with action.

Ernest Hemingway, *Novelist*

Few things can help an individual more than to place responsibility on him, and to let him know that you trust him.

Booker T. Washington, *Educator and Activist*

Raise your words, not voice. It is rain that grows
flowers, not thunder.

Jalal ad-Din Rumi, *Poet*

Some people see things as they are and say
"Why?" I dream things that never were
and say, "Why not?"

George Bernard Shaw, *Playwright*

The ultimate measure of a man is not where
he stands in moments of comfort and convenience,
but where he stands at times of challenge
and controversy.

Martin Luther King, Jr., *Civil Rights Leader*

Tell me and I forget, teach me and I may
remember, involve me and I learn.

Benjamin Franklin, *Statesman and Inventor*

None of us is as smart as all of us.

Kenneth H. Blanchard, *Management Consultant and Author*

Alone we can do so little; together we can do so much.

Helen Keller, *Author and Activist*

Whatever a leader does now sets up what he does later. And there's always a later.

Mike Krzyzewski, *College Basketball Coach*

You can buy a person's hand but you can't buy his heart. His heart is where his enthusiasm, his loyalty is.

Stephen Covey, *Management Consultant and Author*

Start with what is right rather than what is acceptable.

Franz Kafka, *Novelist*

Sometimes it's not strength but gentleness that cracks the hardest shells.

Richard Paul Evans, *Author*

You may have the greatest bunch of individual stars in the world, but if they don't play together, the club won't be worth a dime.

Babe Ruth, *Professional Baseball Player*

A group becomes a team when all members are sure enough of themselves and their contributions to praise the skill of others.

Norman Shidle, *Author*

When you're good at something, you'll tell everyone. When you're great at something, they'll tell you.

Walter Payton, *Professional Football Player*

The greatest good you can do for another is not just share your riches, but to reveal to him his own.

Benjamin Disraeli, *U.K. Prime Minister*

When you're part of a team, you stand up for your teammates. Your loyalty is to them. You protect them through good and bad, because they'd do the same for you.

Yogi Berra, *Professional Baseball Player*

Discovery consists of *seeing* what everyone else has seen and *thinking* what nobody else has thought.

Albert Szent-Györgyi, *Scientist*

The **strength of the team** is each *individual member*. **The strength of each member** is the *team*.

Phil Jackson, *Professional Basketball Player and Coach*

High achievement always takes place in the
framework of high expectation.

Charles F. Kettering, *Businessman and Inventor*

It's no use walking anywhere to preach unless our
walking is our preaching.

St. Francis of Assisi

A leader is a dealer in hope.

Napoleon Bonaparte, *Emperor of France*

Leaders think and talk about the solutions.
Followers think and talk about the problems.

Brian Tracy, *Self-Development Coach and Author*

The greatest leader is not necessarily the one who
does the greatest things. He is the one that gets
people to do the greatest things.

Ronald Reagan, *U.S. President*

The world is moved along, not only by the mighty shoves of its heroes, but also by the aggregate of the tiny pushes of each honest worker.

Helen Keller, *Author and Activist*

The truth of the matter is that you always know the right thing to do. The hard part is doing it.

Norman Schwarzkopf, Jr., *U.S. Army General*

Much can be accomplished by teamwork when no one is concerned about who gets credit.

John Wooden, *College Basketball Coach*

If you want to go fast, go alone. If you want to go far, you have to go with others.

Dale Brown, *College Basketball Coach*

The secret is to work less as individuals and more as a team. As a coach, I play not my eleven best, but my best eleven.

Knute Rockne, *College Football Coach*

Keep away from people who try to belittle your ambitions. Small people always do that, but the really great make you feel that you, too, can become great.

Mark Twain, Novelist

A leader is best when people barely know he exists, when his work is done, his aim fulfilled, they will say: we did it ourselves.

Lao Tzu, *Philosopher*

The best executive is one who has sense enough to pick good men to do what he wants done, and self-restraint to keep from meddling with them while they do it.

Theodore Roosevelt, *U.S. President*

One man's candle is light for many.

Babylonian Talmud, Tractate Shabbat

The best way to predict the future is to create it.

Peter Drucker, *Management Consultant and Author*

If your actions create a legacy that inspires others to dream more, learn more, do more, and become more, you are a leader.

Dolly Parton, *Singer and Songwriter*

Teamwork is the ability to work together toward a common vision.... It is the fuel that allows common people to attain uncommon results.

Andrew Carnegie, *Industrialist and Philanthropist*

Power and influence are effective only when used properly.

James O. Naifeh, *Speaker, Tennessee House of Representatives*

Motivation is the art of getting people to do what you want them to do because they want to do it.

Dwight D. Eisenhower, *U.S. President*

If we all did the things we are capable of doing, we would literally astound ourselves.

Thomas Edison, *Inventor*

Little minds are tamed and subdued by misfortune; but great minds rise above it.

Washington Irving, *Author*

Coming together is a beginning, staying together is progress, and working together is success.

Henry Ford, *Founder, Ford Motor Company*

Give

There are two kinds of people in the world: givers and takers. *The takers may eat better, but the givers* sleep better.

Danny Thomas, *Founder, St. Jude Children's Research Hospital, Entertainer, and Humanitarian*

You give but little when you give of your possessions. *It is when you give of yourself that you truly give.*

Khalil Gibran, *Poet and Philosopher*

A candle loses nothing by lighting another candle.

James Keller, *Roman Catholic Priest*

It is in spending oneself that one becomes rich.

Sarah Bernhardt, *Actress*

The smallest act of kindness is worth more than the grandest intention.

Oscar Wilde, *Playwright*

To whom much is given, much is expected.

Luke 12:48

Give and you shall receive, much more than you would have ever thought possible. Give, give again and again, don't lose courage, keep it up and go on giving! No one has ever become poor from giving.

Anne Frank, *Diarist*

We can't help everyone, but everyone can help someone.

Ronald Reagan, *U.S. President*

The sage does not accumulate for himself. The more he uses for others, the more he has himself. The more he gives away, the more he possesses of his own.

Lao Tzu, *Philosopher*

There is a wonderful mythical law of nature that the three things we crave most in life — happiness, freedom, and peace of mind — are always attained by giving them to someone else.

Peyton C. March, *U.S. Army Chief of Staff*

No matter what you decide to do with your life, you will glorify God if you do something to help your fellow man.

Joseph S. Azar, Sr., *Realtor*

The greatest use of life is to spend it for something that will outlast it.

William James, *Philosopher and Psychologist*

If you can't feed a hundred people, then feed just one.

Mother Teresa, *Roman Catholic Saint*

The best way to find yourself is to lose yourself in the service of others.

Mahatma Gandhi, *Indian Political and Spiritual Leader*

If you want to lift yourself up, lift up someone else.

Booker T. Washington, *Educator and Activist*

Do your little bit of good where you are; it is those little bits of good put together that overwhelm the world.

Desmond Tutu, *Anglican Bishop and Human Rights Activist*

It may be true that no good deed goes unpunished, but I am not afraid of punishment so I keep trying to do good deeds.

Thomas DeSimone, *Real Estate Developer*

There are those who give with joy, and that joy is their reward. And there are those who give with pain, and that pain is their baptism.

Khalil Gibran, *Poet and Philosopher*

If you want others to be happy, practice
compassion. If you want to be happy,
practice compassion.

Tenzin Gyatso, *The 14th Dalai Lama of Tibet*

Service to others is the rent you pay for your room
here on earth.

Muhammad Ali, *Professional Boxer*

You will not attain righteousness till you spend in
charity of the things you love.

Quran (3:92)

We make a living by what we get, but we make a life
by what we give.

Winston Churchill, *U.K. Prime Minister*

Those who exalt themselves will be humbled, and
those who humble themselves will be exalted.

Luke 14:11 and Matthew 23:12

A man has made at least a start on discovering the meaning of human life when he plants shade trees under which he knows full well he will never sit.

D. Elton Trueblood, *Theologian*

Carve your name on hearts, not tombstones. A legacy is etched into the minds of others and the stories they share about you.

Shannon L. Alder, *Author*

Only a life lived for others is worthwhile.

Albert Einstein, *Physicist*

Great opportunities to help others seldom come, but small ones surround us every day.

Sally Koch, *Author*

The miracle is this: the more we share the more we have.

Leonard Nimoy, *Actor*

A man wrapped up
in himself makes a
very small bundle.

Benjamin Franklin, *Statesman and Inventor*

What counts in life is
not the mere fact that we
have lived. It is **what
difference we have made in
the lives of others** that will
determine the significance
of the life we lead.

Nelson Mandela, *President of South Africa*

I believe that every right implies a responsibility;
every opportunity, an obligation; every possession,
a duty.

John D. Rockefeller, Jr., *Industrialist and Philanthropist*

I long to accomplish a great and noble task, but
it is my chief duty to accomplish humble tasks as
though they were great and noble.

Helen Keller, *Author and Activist*

How wonderful it is that nobody need wait a single
moment before starting to improve the world.

Anne Frank, *Diarist*

To do more for the world than the world does for
you — that is success.

Henry Ford, *Founder, Ford Motor Company*

Never reach out your hand unless you're willing to
extend an arm.

Pope Paul VI

Go into the world and do well. But more importantly, go into the world and do good.

Minor Myers, Jr., *Illinois Wesleyan University President*

No one is useless in this world who lightens the burdens of another.

Charles Dickens, *Novelist*

I don't know what your destiny will be, but one thing I do know: the only ones among you who will be really happy are those who have sought and found how to serve.

Albert Schweitzer, *Theologian*

Never believe that a few caring people can't change the world. For, indeed, that's all who ever have.

Margaret Mead, *Anthropologist*

What counts can't always be counted; what can be counted doesn't always count.

Albert Einstein, *Physicist*

Nobody is ever impoverished through the giving of charity.

Maimonides, *Philosopher and Scholar*

The price of greatness is responsibility.

Winston Churchill, *U.K. Prime Minister*

Care and Love

A good relationship has a pattern like a dance and is built on some of the same rules. The partners do not need to hold on tightly, because they move confidently in the same pattern, intricate but gay and *swift and free*, like a country dance of Mozart's.

Anne Morrow Lindbergh, *Author and Aviator*

I would rather **walk with a friend in the dark**, than *alone in the light*.

Helen Keller, *Author and Activist*

You may forget with whom you laughed, but you will never forget with whom you wept.

Khalil Gibran, *Poet and Philosopher*

You know you're in love when you can't fall asleep because reality is finally better than your dreams.

Dr. Seuss, *Author*

A friend is one that knows you as you are, understands where you have been, accepts what you have become, and helps to get you where you want to go.

Unknown

Surround yourself only with people who are going to lift you higher.

Oprah Winfrey, *Talk Show Host, Philanthropist, and Actress*

I've learned that people will forget what you said, people will forget what you did, but people will never forget how you made them feel.

Maya Angelou, *Poet*

We all take different paths in life, but no matter where we go, we take a little of each other everywhere.

Tim McGraw, *Singer and Actor*

How far you go in life depends on your being tender with the young, compassionate with the aged, sympathetic with the striving, and tolerant of the weak and strong. Because someday in your life you will have been all of these.

George Washington Carver, *Scientist*

If you judge people, you have no time to love them.

Mother Teresa, *Roman Catholic Saint*

For the man who prays in his heart, the whole world is a church.

Silouan the Athonite, *Eastern Orthodox Monk and Saint*

To handle yourself, use your head; to handle others, use your heart.

Eleanor Roosevelt, *U.S. First Lady, Diplomat, and Social Activist*

What we have once enjoyed deeply we can never lose. All that we love deeply becomes a part of us.

Helen Keller, *Author and Activist*

Remember the world is built in a circle.

Salem Abraham, *Investment Manager*

If you can't handle me at my worst, then you sure as hell don't deserve me at my best.

Marilyn Monroe, *Actress*

If you really love something set it free; if it comes back it's yours, if it doesn't, it never was.

Richard Bach, *Novelist*

The most precious gift we can offer anyone is our attention.

Thich Nhat Hanh, *Author and Buddhist Monk*

Tell me whom you walk with and I will tell you who you are.

Spanish Proverb

You can give without loving, but you cannot love without giving.

Robert Louis Stevenson, *Novelist*

A real friend is one who walks in when the rest of the world walks out.

Walter Winchell, *Television and Radio Broadcaster*

The greatest weapon against stress is our ability to choose one thought over another.

William James, *Philosopher and Psychologist*

Friends love through all kinds of weather, and families stick together in all kinds of trouble.

Proverbs 17:17

For it was not into my ear you whispered, but into my heart. It was not my lips you kissed, but my soul.

Judy Garland, *Singer and Actress*

A successful marriage requires falling in love many times, always with the same person.

Mignon McLaughlin, *Journalist and Author*

My true religion is kindness.

Tenzin Gyatso, *The 14th Dalai Lama of Tibet*

Comparison is the thief of joy.

Theodore Roosevelt, *U.S. President*

Remember not only to say the right thing in the right place, but far more difficult still, to leave unsaid the wrong thing at the tempting moment.

Benjamin Franklin, *Statesman and Inventor*

I love you not only for what you are, but for what I am when I'm with you.

Roy Croft, *Poet*

Let us always meet each other with smile, for the smile is the beginning of love.

Mother Teresa, *Roman Catholic Saint*

Two mountains can't come together, but *two people* can.

Yiddish Proverb

Don't walk behind me; I may not lead. Don't walk in front of me; I may not follow. *Just walk beside me and be my friend.*

Albert Camus, *Novelist and Philosopher*

View marriage as a 100% - 0% arrangement.
Make a commitment that you will give 100%
and expect nothing in return. If you do, you
will view everything you receive from your spouse
as a gift of love.

George Simon, *Entrepreneur Industrialist*

The consciousness of loving and being loved brings
a warmth and richness to life that nothing else
can bring.

Oscar Wilde, *Playwright*

Friends are those rare people who ask how we are,
and then wait to hear the answer.

Ed Cunningham, *Professional Football Player*

Kindness is a language which the deaf can hear and
the blind can see.

Mark Twain, *Novelist*

God could not be everywhere and therefore he
made mothers.

Rudyard Kipling, *Novelist and Poet*

Any man can be a father, but it takes someone special to be a Dad.

Anne Geddes, *Photographer*

A happy family is but an earlier heaven.

George Bernard Shaw, *Playwright*

The best and most beautiful things in the world cannot be seen or even touched — they must be felt within the heart.

Helen Keller, *Author and Activist*

When I hear somebody sigh, "Life is hard," I am always tempted to ask, "Compared to what?"

Sydney J. Harris, *Journalist*

Be kind, for everyone you meet is fighting a hard battle.

Ian Maclaren, *Author and Theologian*

A kind deed for someone may be appreciated;
a kind deed for someone's child will never
be forgotten.

Joseph S. Ayoub, Sr., *Attorney, Father, and Grandfather*

Family is not an important thing. It is everything.

Michael J. Fox, *Actor and Activist*

Let others confide in you. It may not help you, but
it surely will help them.

Roger Imhoff, *Author*

For attractive lips, speak words of kindness. For
lovely eyes, seek out the good in people…. For
poise, walk with the knowledge that you'll never
walk alone.

Sam Levenson, *Humorist and Television Host*

A single act of kindness throws out roots in
all directions, and the roots spring up and make
new trees.

Amelia Earhart, *Aviation Pioneer and Author*

You can't touch love, but you can feel the sweetness that it pours into everything.

Anne Sullivan, *Teacher*

Kind words can be short and easy to speak, but their echoes are truly endless.

Mother Teresa, *Roman Catholic Saint*

Never ruin an apology with an excuse.

Benjamin Franklin, *Statesman and Inventor*

A friend is someone who knows the song in your heart and can sing it back to you when you have forgotten the words.

C.S. Lewis, *Novelist and Literary Critic*

Lord, please help me to be a blessing to anyone I come in contact with today.

David Rosenberg, *Business Executive*

Kisses are Band-Aids for the world.

Larissa May, *Blogger and Founder of @halfthestory*

Absence is to love what wind is to fire; it extinguishes the small, it inflames the great.

Roger de Bussy-Rabutin, *Writer*

Find Peace

It is often in the darkest skies we see the *brightest stars.*

Richard Evans, *Author*

Stop and *remember* nice things.

Dempsey John Brockelman, *1994-1999*

Neuroblastoma Patient, Old Soul

If we magnified blessings as much as we magnify disappointments, we would all be much happier.

John Wooden, *College Basketball Coach*

We can never obtain peace in the outer world until we make peace with ourselves.

Tenzin Gyatso, *The 14th Dalai Lama of Tibet*

Getting over a painful experience is much like crossing monkey bars. You have to let go at some point in order to move forward.

C.S. Lewis, *Novelist and Literary Critic*

A man with one watch knows what time it is; a man with two watches is never sure what time it is.

Chinese Proverb

Holding onto anger is like taking a poison and expecting the other person to die.

Buddha

True Story, Word of Honor: Joseph Heller, an important and funny writer now dead, and I were at a party given by a billionaire on Shelter Island. I said, "Joe, how does it make you feel to know that our host only yesterday may have made more money than your novel *Catch-22* has earned in its entire history?" And Joe said, "I've got something he can never have." And I said, "What on earth could that be, Joe?" And Joe said, "The knowledge that I've got enough." Not bad! Rest in Peace!

Kurt Vonnegut, *Novelist*

If you concentrate on finding whatever is good in every situation, you will discover that your life will suddenly be filled with gratitude, a feeling that nurtures the soul.

Harold Kushner, *Rabbi and Author*

Accept what is, let go of what was, and have faith in what will be.

Sonia Ricotti, *Motivational Speaker and Author*

It is better to light one candle than to curse the darkness.

Chinese Proverb

It's not what happens to you, but how you react to it that matters.

Epictetus, *Philosopher*

New beginnings are often disguised as painful endings.

Lao Tzu, *Philosopher*

Happiness is not a state to arrive at, but a manner of traveling.

Margaret Lee Runbeck, *Author*

I like the dreams of the future better than the history of the past.

Thomas Jefferson, *U.S. President*

Tough times don't last. Tough people do.

Gregory Peck, *Actor*

Never get so fascinated by the extraordinary that you forget ordinary.

Magdalen Nabb, *Author*

When you are paralyzed by fear, invite curiosity in, they can't live in your brain at the same time.

Ruth Gaviria, *Marketing Executive*

The art of being happy lies in the power of extracting happiness from common things.

Henry Ward Beecher, *Minister and Abolitionist*

A pessimist sees the difficulty in every opportunity; an optimist sees the opportunity in every difficulty.

Attributed to Winston Churchill, *U.K. Prime Minister*

Be thankful for what you have; you'll end up having more. If you concentrate on what you don't have, you will never, ever have enough.

Oprah Winfrey, *Talk Show Host, Philanthropist, and Actress*

Out of suffering have emerged the strongest souls; the most massive characters are seared with scars.

Khalil Gibran, *Poet and Philosopher*

Life's challenges are not supposed to paralyze you, they're supposed to help you discover who you are.

Bernice Johnson Reagon, *Singer and Social Activist*

In three words I can sum up everything I've learned about life: it goes on.

Robert Frost, *Poet*

The greatest discovery of all time is that a person can change his future by merely changing his attitude.

Oprah Winfrey, *Talk Show Host, Philanthropist, and Actress*

Every thought is a seed. If you plant crab apples, don't count on harvesting golden delicious.

Bill Meyer, *Professional Baseball Player and Manager*

The more concerned we become over the things we can't control, the less we will do with the things we can control.

John Wooden, *College Basketball Coach*

Every blade of grass
has its **angel** that bends
over it and whispers,
"grow, grow."

Midrash Genesis Rabbah

When you are sorrowful
look again in your heart,
and you shall see that
in **truth** you are weeping
for that which has been
your delight.

Khalil Gibran, *Poet and Philosopher*

God grant me the serenity to accept the things I cannot change, the courage to change the things I can, and the wisdom to know the difference.

Reinhold Niebuhr, *Theologian*

If God did not exist, it would be necessary to invent him.

Voltaire, *Philosopher*

I believe in pink. I believe that laughing is the best calorie burner. I believe in kidding a lot. I believe in being strong when everything seems to be going wrong. I believe that happy girls are the prettiest girls. I believe that tomorrow is another day and I believe in miracles.

Audrey Hepburn, *Actress and Humanitarian*

Let go or be dragged.

Zen Proverb

It is foolish and wrong to mourn the men who died. Rather we should thank God that such men lived.

George S. Patton, *U.S. Army General*

It never gets darker than midnight.

Rocco Fazzolari, *Italian Farmer and U.S. Immigrant*

Some people see scars, and it is wounding they
remember. To me they are proof of the fact that
there is healing.

Linda Hogan, *Poet and Storyteller*

A smile is a curve that sets everything straight.

Phyllis Diller, *Comedian*

Faith is being sure of what we hope for and certain
of what we do not see.

Hebrews 11:1

I have sometimes been wildly, despairingly, acutely
miserable, racked with sorrow, but through it all I
still know quite certainly that just to be alive is
a grand thing.

Agatha Christie, *Mystery Novelist*

He who wants a rose must respect the thorn.

Persian Proverb

Your present circumstances don't determine where you can go; they merely determine where you start.

Nido R. Qubein, *Businessman and Educator*

Keep your thoughts positive, because your thoughts become your words. Keep your words positive, because your words become your behavior. Keep your behavior positive, because your behavior becomes your habits. Keep your habits positive, because your habits become your values. Keep your values positive, because your values become your destiny.

Mahatma Gandhi, *Indian Political and Spiritual Leader*

Grief is the price we pay for love.

Queen Elizabeth II

Now and then it is good to pause in our pursuit of happiness and just be happy.

Guillaume Apollinaire, *Poet*

Fill each day with life and heart. There is no pleasure in the world comparable to the delight and satisfaction that a good person takes in doing good.

John Tillotson, *Archbishop of Canterbury*

For every minute you are angry you lose sixty seconds of happiness.

Ralph Waldo Emerson, *Essayist and Poet*

Some people are always grumbling because roses have thorns; I am thankful that thorns have roses.

Jean-Baptiste Alphonse Karr

If you want the rainbow, you have to put up with the rain.

Dolly Parton, *Singer and Songwriter*

Worry does not empty tomorrow of its sorrow, it empties today of its strength.

Corrie Ten Boom, *Activist and Author*

When angry, count ten before you speak; if very angry, a hundred.

Thomas Jefferson, *U.S. President*

I discovered I always have choices and sometimes it's only a choice of attitude.

Judith Knowlton, *Author*

Don't cry because it is over, smile because it happened.

Dr. Seuss, *Author*

Smile and Laugh

It is the ability to
take a joke, not make one,
that proves you have
a sense of humor.

Max Eastman, *Writer and Political Activist*

Laughter is the sun
that drives winter from
the human face.

Victor Hugo, *Novelist*

I would challenge you to a battle of wits, but I see you are unarmed.

William Shakespeare, *Playwright and Poet*

No need to rush to a wake, he isn't going anywhere.

Joseph S. Ayoub, Sr., *Attorney, Father, and Grandfather*

She said she was approaching forty, and I couldn't help wondering from what direction.

Bob Hope, *Entertainer*

I asked God for a bike, but I know God doesn't work that way. So I stole a bike and asked for forgiveness.

Emo Philips, *Comedian*

I don't suffer from insanity, I enjoy every minute of it.

Edgar Allen Poe, *Author*

I couldn't wait for success so I went ahead without it.

Jonathan Winters, *Comedian*

Ice cream is exquisite. What a pity it isn't illegal.

Voltaire, *Philosopher*

At every party, there are two kinds of people — those who want to go home and those who don't. The trouble is, they are usually married to each other.

Ann Landers, *Columnist*

Always borrow money from a pessimist. He won't expect it back.

Oscar Wilde, *Playwright*

Depend on the rabbit's foot if you will, but remember: it didn't work for the rabbit.

R.E. Shay, *Humorist*

There can't be a crisis next week. My schedule
is already full.

Henry Kissinger, *U.S. Secretary of State*

The Torrah says, love your neighbor as yourself.
The Buddha says, there is no self. So, maybe we're
off the hook.

Unknown

If at first you don't succeed, then skydiving is
not for you.

Steven Wright, *Comedian*

If you obey all the rules, you'll miss all the fun.

Katharine Hepburn, *Actress*

A committee is a group that keeps minutes and
loses hours.

Milton Berle, *Comedian*

I'm on a whiskey diet. I've lost three days already!

Tommy Cooper, *Comedian*

If you haven't got anything nice to say about anybody, come sit next to me.

Alice Roosevelt Longworth, *Writer and Socialite*

I once spent a year in Philadelphia. I think it was on a Sunday.

W.C. Fields, *Comedian*

Always look out for Number One and be careful not to step in Number Two.

Rodney Dangerfield, *Comedian*

The problem with winning the rat race is you're still a rat.

Lily Tomlin, *Comedian and Actress*

When in charge, ponder. When in trouble, delegate. When in doubt, mumble.

James Boren, *Humorist*

A few words from Yogi Berra

Professional Baseball Player

A nickel ain't worth a dime anymore.

Never answer an anonymous letter.

He hits from both sides of the plate.
He's amphibious.

The towels were so thick there I could hardly
close my suitcase.

You should always go to other people's funerals;
otherwise, they won't come to yours.

When you come to a fork in the road, take it.

Little League baseball is a very good thing
because it keeps the parents off the streets.

The future ain't what it used to be.

Nobody goes there anymore. It's too crowded.

Nobody ever **died**
of *laughter*.

Max Beerbohm, *Humorist*

Do not take life
too seriously. You will
never get out of it alive.

Elbert G. Hubbard, *Writer and Artist*

If I'd known I was gonna live this long, I'd have taken better care of myself.

Eubie Blake, *Musician*

Knowledge is knowing a tomato is a fruit; wisdom is not putting it in a fruit salad.

Miles Kington, *Journalist and Broadcaster*

Be sure to laugh every day. If you don't, you need new friends.

Mark Crandall, *Banker*

I can resist everything except temptation.

Oscar Wilde, *Playwright*

If you find yourself in a hole, stop digging.

Will Rogers, *Humorist*

When I turned two I was really anxious, because I'd doubled my age in a year. I thought, if this keeps up, by the time I'm six I'll be ninety.

Steven Wright, *Comedian*

A man's got to believe in something. I believe I'll have another drink.

W.C. Fields, *Comedian*

Some cause happiness wherever they go; others, whenever they go.

Oscar Wilde, *Playwright*

I'm at an age when my back goes out more than I do.

Phyllis Diller, *Comedian*

If everybody was as smart as you are, you wouldn't be so smart.

Joseph S. Ayoub, Sr., *Attorney, Father, and Grandfather*

Talk to people about themselves and they will listen for hours.

Benjamin Disraeli, *U.K. Prime Minister*

After hearing all those comments and accolades, I feel obligated to die.

Lewis Donelson, *Attorney*

To get something done, a committee should consist of no more than three people, two of whom are absent.

Robert Copeland, *Writer*

I intend to live forever. So far, so good.

Steven Wright, *Comedian*

The best after-dinner speech I ever heard was, "Waiter, I'll take the check."

Adlai Stevenson II, *Illinois Governor and U.S. Ambassador*

Everyone has a book in them and that, in most cases, is where the book should stay.

Christopher Hitchens, *Author and Journalist*

Ladies and gentlemen:
The subject may not be
exhausted, but *we are*.

George Bernard Shaw, *Playwright*

About the Photographs

What is dark yet made with light? A shadow.

"Everything we see projects a parallel version of itself, a chorus in plain view that sings volumes about our world," expressed Mitch Weiss as we discussed the genesis of his series of photographs titled #mwshadow. He went on to explain that, "interpreting a shadow before the form is akin to listening before speaking." Once I appreciated the subtlety of this distinction, it elucidated a connection between his series and the contents of this book.

As we consume the quotes that fill these pages, the photographs that introduce each chapter remind us that some insights and wisdom can only be found in the reflection and study our own perspectives bring to life. In the pictures, Weiss captures mindfully observed, naturally occurring shadows that reveal irony, humor, pareidolia, and unexpected geometry. In the quotes filling each chapter, the authors and orators similarly capture a unique perspective on life, one that causes us to pause, think, and inspires us to see the world a little differently.

Attribution of Sources

We believe that each quotation in this book should stand on its own, regardless of the source or author. We hope that you will savor each quotation as if you were tasting a great wine without first having read the label. It is the words that provide the power and impact, not the person who might have originally written or spoken the words.

We recognize, however, that the source provides interesting context. Thus, we have made an effort to accurately attribute each quotation to its original source. For most quotes, the source is definitive. However, in researching the quotations in this book, we were surprised to learn that many had multiple potential authors or were commonly misattributed. In those cases, we used the following guiding principles:

We attributed the quotation to the person or source dating furthest back in time. If there were two or more potential sources from the same time period, we attributed the quote to the source most closely associated with it. For quotations for which these guidelines did not yield an appropriate or clear attribution, or in cases when the source was ambiguous at best, we declared the source as "unknown." Also, when the source of the quotation was an individual writing under a pseudonym, we only used the pseudonym (*i.e.*, George Eliot [Mary Ann Evans], Dr. Seuss [Theodor Geisel], Victoria Holt [Eleanor Hibbert], and Mark Twain [Samuel Clemens]).

Description of Sources

We have provided a brief description of all attributed sources. When the source was an individual, we described the person generally by occupation, role, or most notable contribution to society. If there was a single job or position that defined the person, we used that job or position title.

In cases where there were several options for a description, we chose what would commonly be considered the dominant role, occupation or contribution. When more appropriate, we used multiple descriptors. We tried to limit the description to five or fewer words, starting with the most significant descriptor.

For those persons less well known or not previously published, we described them as they would most likely describe themselves as of this writing or, in the case of those not living, how they or others would have described them when they were alive.

The descriptions are not intended to be a resume nor are they intended to provide a political or other editorial statement about the source. We invite the reader to further research the source of any quotation as, for many sources, a few words cannot do full justice.

In limited cases, we did not use a description because we determined that the source was self-explanatory in the name of the source itself.

Acknowledgments

We would like to thank some special people who made significant contributions to *Inspire Me!*

First, we want to acknowledge the author of the Foreword of this book, Jane Cronin Ayoub. Inspiring as a wife, mother, and individual, Jane has been the backbone of this book and our lives. She encouraged and advised us every step of the way and has been as much a contributor to this book as anyone. Every quote about love, friendship, support, and helping others is an appropriate way to describe Jane!

Meghan Kelly, our Director of Research, has worked tirelessly helping us compile, review, screen, and curate thousands of quotations. She has been an integral part of our team from the first day. Her energy, passion, vision, spirit, and commitment to *Inspire Me!* have been inspiring to all of us. Meghan has been a driving force for this project for which we are deeply grateful.

The Humble Hues team consisting of Michael Winston, Mitchell Weiss, and Kate Terrado, like any publishing group, was individually and collectively invaluable. Their wisdom, experience, and guidance in working with us to conceptualize and produce *Inspire Me!*, including organizing the content and navigating the publishing process, have been essential. Michael's professional business sense, Mitch's amazing photographic eye and Kate's artistic prowess are all individually impressive; together they are an unparalleled combination of talent.

Maria McDonough patiently, steadfastly and effectively kept the numerous and varied moving parts of the process of producing

Inspire Me! organized and progressing in a seemingly effortless way — just as she does with all we do together every day. An ever-calming force, Maria greeted each challenge with a reassuring smile and cool resolve. Her contribution cannot be overstated.

Liz Cronin Urban and Michael D. Urban graciously dedicated an immense amount of time throughout the entire process of compiling quotations, meticulously editing this book, passionately and enthusiastically researching and verifying attribution of quotes, including some of the more difficult ones. Who knew that John Quincy Adams was wrongly attributed as the source of a quote originated by Dolly Parton: "We cannot direct the wind, but we can adjust the sails"? Similarly, Joe and Christa Ayoub were generous with their time, working with us to evaluate each quotation for inclusion along with the proper attributions and descriptions of the authors.

Rob Fox was instrumental in the final stages of our editing process, lending his vast literary knowledge to provide a greatly-appreciated comprehensive review and critical eye to this book. We also are appreciative of the editorial guidance we received from Jeanne Blake and Maura King Scully, and the work of our research team consisting of Stephanie Calnan, Meghan Mahder, Tyler Patterson, and Jason Oneida. We also thank Michael Bohnen for his assistance in researching and properly attributing the source of some of the more difficult quotations.

Many others made valuable contributions.

Emily Callahan and Judy Habib were enormously supportive, especially at the conceptualization stage of this book, in helping us find the right focus and format of *Inspire Me!*, given our goals and objectives for this book.

Also instrumental at the conceptualization stage and in understanding how best to compile, produce, and promote *Inspire Me!* were Shelly O'Neill, Ann Murphy, Cosmo Macero, Jr., and the other members of the O'Neill and Associates team. We valued their support and insight in the formative stages of this book. We also deeply appreciate their generosity in all they will be doing to help us promote *Inspire Me!* and raise funds for St. Jude Children's Research Hospital through the sale of this book.

We also thank Stephen Saber for providing his publishing experience and strategic insights in helping us to define, develop, and execute on our publishing and marketing strategy.

Wendy Fiscus, Judy Habib, Katheryn Kelly, Jay and Kara Paganelli, Marianne Pesaturo, Alex Rouleau, and Mike and Mary Beth Zabowsky, along with Maria McDonough, Liz Cronin Urban, and Michael D. Urban, were part of our focus group that helped us screen quotations, an exercise that required many hours from each of them. Their guidance motivated us to continue and reaffirmed our sense that there was value in publishing this book.

A number of friends and colleagues contributed quotes of their own.

They have been acknowledged in the preceding pages where their quotes appear. Several people contributed favorite quotations of others, and we gratefully acknowledge each of them, to the extent that they did not contribute a personal quotation as well: Susan Aguillard, Nikki Ayoub, Fred Azar, Peter and Wendy Brockelman, Michael Burke, Stephen Camer, Haley Cassriel, Peter Chow, Marika Crowe, John Fish, Rob Fox, Gabriel Haddad, Charles Hajjar, Fouad Hajjar, Michael Hussey, Katheryn Kelly, Tori Mahon, Doug MacLean, Vic Paci, Tom Penn, Marianne Pesaturo, Joseph G. Shaker, George Simon, Paul Simon, Liz Cronin Urban, Michael D. Urban, Paul Wein, and Mike Zabowsky.

A special note from Paul: I want to acknowledge my colleagues at Nutter, McClennen & Fish. I joined Nutter in no small part because of the firm's history and commitment to making a difference in the world. Founded in 1879 by U. S. Supreme Court Justice Louis D. Brandeis, the firm stands for providing exceptional legal counsel with an unwavering dedication to the success of our clients. Additionally, Nutter continues to this day to honor Brandeis' commitment to active participation in community service. The firm has steadfastly supported my commitment to ALSAC/St. Jude Children's Research Hospital from the first day I arrived. As my involvement has deepened, so has the support and embrace of Nutter. Although each member of the firm plays an important role, our Managing Partner, Deborah Manus, deserves special recognition for supporting and promoting our firm's culture and core values.

To all of the above, we say thank you for all you did and thank you for inspiring us.

About St. Jude Children's Research Hospital

The mission of St. Jude Children's Research Hospital is to find cures for children with cancer and other life-threatening diseases through research and treatment. St. Jude is dedicated to the belief of founder Danny Thomas that "No child should die in the dawn of life." It is a hospital, unlike any other, where cutting-edge research is brought together with extraordinary patient care and unparalleled family support. St. Jude is turning laboratory breakthroughs into lifesaving treatments for children — every day.

Doctors and researchers at St. Jude are leading the way the world understands, treats, and defeats childhood cancer and other life-threatening diseases. Unlike any other hospital, the majority of funding for St. Jude comes from individual contributions. Thanks to generous donors, families never receive a bill from St. Jude for treatment, travel, housing or food — because all a family should worry about is helping their child live. Treatments invented at St. Jude have helped push the overall childhood cancer survival rate in the U.S. from 20 percent, when the hospital opened its doors in 1962, to 80 percent today. St. Jude's research laboratories may not be in your community — but their discoveries are. Part of the national and global power of St. Jude is that it freely shares the discoveries it makes, and every child saved at St. Jude means doctors and scientists worldwide can use that knowledge to save thousands more children.

All profits from this book will be donated to St. Jude Children's Research Hospital.

Colophon

Bodoni is used as the primary typeface of this book. Bodoni is the name given to the serif typefaces first designed by Giambattista Bodoni in the late 18th century. Massimo Vignelli stated that "Bodoni is one of the most elegant typefaces ever designed." The secondary typeface is Whitney, a 20th-century design by American type designer Tobias Frere-Jones.

The juxtaposition of these typefaces — old and new, serif and sans-serif — speaks to the depth, breadth, and variety of this curated collection of quotations.

Paul Ayoub is a partner and serves on the Executive Committee of the law firm of Nutter, McClennen & Fish LLP in Boston, Massachusetts, and represents a wide variety of for profit and not-for-profit organizations. A graduate of Brown University and Boston College Law School, Paul currently serves as the Chair of the national Board of Directors of ALSAC, the fundraising and awareness organization for St. Jude Children's Research Hospital in Memphis, Tennessee. Locally, Paul serves as Vice Chair of the Board of Directors of the Greater Boston Chamber of Commerce and on several other not-for-profit boards.

Lizzie Ayoub is a consulting analyst for a global technology and management consulting company in its Atlanta, Georgia office. She is a graduate of Noble and Greenough School and Vanderbilt University with a degree in Human and Organizational Development. In middle school and high school, Lizzie combined her two passions of singing and St. Jude by recording and selling a CD, with all proceeds going to the Hospital. She also has performed at St. Jude fundraising events around the country.

Dr. Seuss

Arnold Palmer

Agatha Christie

Ayn Rand

B. Franklin

Bertrand Russell

C. S. Lewis

Vincent

T. Carlyle

Thomas A. Edison

Rudyard Kipling

Th. Jefferson

T. S. Eliot

Bacon

Mark Twain

John Wayne

Steven Jobs

Teresa

Lincoln

Judy Garland

Anne Fran

Alber   Brian I

A. E. Thinson

Coco Chanel

W. B. Yeats

Walt Whitman

Woodrow Wilson

Jonathan Wi

Theodore Roosevelt

Robert

Parker   S. Hawking   Isaac

Hugo   Asimov

Mandela   Margaret

Elizabeth R

Martin Luther King Jr.